NOTES ON EPHESIANS

James Poole

ISBN: 978-1-78364-303-5

THE OPEN BIBLE TRUST
Fordland Mount, Upper Basildon,
Reading, RG8 8LU, UK.

www.obt.org.uk

NOTES ON EPHESIANS

Contents

Introduction: A simple analysis of Ephesians

Introduction: A simple analysis of Ephesians

- Salutation (1:1-2)
    - o Our standing in Christ (1:3-3:19
- Doxology (3:20-21)
    - o Our walk in Christ (4:1-6:20)
- Benediction (6:21-24)

At the close of the book of Acts the Apostle Paul, a prisoner in Rome, pronounced a solemn declaration of judicial spiritual blindness upon the nation of Israel which had repeatedly rejected their Messiah, Jesus Christ (Acts 28:26-28). This was a quotation from Isaiah 6:9-10, and it had already been spoken by our Lord in Matthew 13:14-15. He foreknew the outcome of the testimony of the Twelve apostles and Paul, that Israel would not listen. Henceforth, the salvation of God was to be sent *direct* to the Gentile nations.

In AD 70 the Roman Emperor Titus destroyed the city of Jerusalem and its temple. He massacred the Jews and Israel became *lo-ammi* (not My people).

Many Christians today say that the church which is the Body of Christ has replaced Israel, that it is the "new Israel" and has inherited the promises given to Abraham concerning Israel (Genesis 12:1-3). I cannot agree with this. The Bible nowhere states that the particular privileges and responsibilities of Israel would be given to anyone else – neither another nation, nor the Church the Body of Christ. In fact, the Scriptures emphatically state that Israel will be restored to fulfil her destiny, with repentance and acknowledgment of Christ her Messiah. (Compare Genesis 12:1-3; Jeremiah 31:31-37; Romans 11:15, 25-29.)

God's purpose concerning Israel has come to a temporary halt. In its place God has given to mankind the gospel of His grace concerning His

Son – see the Epistle to the Romans. [1] In the Ephesian epistle we see that, for nearly 2,000 years, He has been calling out believers to form the Body of Christ whose ultimate destiny is to be in the heavenly realms, blessed with all spiritual blessings in Christ (Ephesians 1:3). This is the theme of these notes and it will help the reader to have a Bible open as he considers them. May they be a great source of blessing.

These notes are based on the *King James Authorised Version*, duly amended where the Greek requires a finer shade of meaning.

---

[1] For more on this see *Romans: Background and Introduction* by Brian Sherring, published by The Open Bible Trust

Ephesians 1

Ephesians 1

Verse 1:   The texts read "Christ Jesus" in both cases. This title points to His exaltation, while "Jesus Christ" engages us with His humiliation. Christ Jesus is used many times by Paul in his epistles. Paul met Him in a blaze of glory on the Damascus road and was blinded for three days (Acts 9:3, 8-9).

"At Ephesus" is omitted by some ancient manuscripts, and it would appear that copies of the epistle were made and sent to all of Paul's churches, including Ephesus.

Verse 2:   "Grace and peace". Note the order. The source is "God our Father", and the channel through which they come to us is "the Lord Jesus Christ". In verses 3-14, Paul, in breathless praise, recounts the blessings that are ours, as members of the Body of Christ.

Verse 3:   "Spiritual blessings in heavenly places in Christ". The realm of all our spiritual blessings is heavenly. The word "places" is in italics in the *KJV* indicating it is not in the original; literally, it is "in the heavenlies". This includes not only places but also heavenly beings. We are blessed among the highest dignitaries in heaven in Christ.

Verse 4: "He (the Father) has chosen us in Him (the Son)". We are a gift from the Father to His Son (John 6:37). Why did the Father choose us? To be sure, we have no merit in ourselves! The choice of Israel was because He loved them (Deuteronomy 7:7-8), and so it is with us!

"Before the foundation of the world". The Greek word for "foundation", is *themelios*, but in this verse the Greek is *katabole*, from which we get our English word "catabolism", meaning destructive metabolism. Sin did not begin with Adam, for Satan had fallen earlier. Scripture tells us that there was a rebellion amongst the angels (2 Peter 2:4; Jude 6) and Satan headed that rebellion (Ezekiel 28:12-15). In the resulting judgment, "the earth was (became) waste and void", (Genesis 1:2 *NIV* margin).

Thus we were chosen in Christ before sin entered the universe" ... that we should be holy and without blame before Him, in love." We are, even now, holy and flawless in His sight. This is how God the Father sees us in His Son! When Christ is manifested in glory, and we with Him (Colossians 3:4), our state in Christ will completely match our standing in Him! The Father's view of us in His Son is timeless – past, present and future!

Punctuation in Scripture is not inspired. We can, with liberty, put the words "in love", which come at the end of verse 4, to the beginning of verse 5. The word "love" links up with the Father's choice and predestination of us.

Verses 5-6: "According to the good pleasure (delight) of His will". This is the "reason" why we were predestined "unto the adoption of children" (Greek *huios* = son), placed as sons with all the benefits of such an "adoption by Jesus Christ to Himself." Such glorifies His grace, "wherein He has made us accepted in the Beloved" (literally, graced us in the Son of His love!).

Verse 7: "...the forgiveness of sins according to the riches of His grace." Sin is a falling short of a standard of righteousness acceptable in God's sight. It is also a transgression, the breaking of God's Law. Its deepest sense is that it is an offence against God's feelings, in His heart! Hence, the forgiveness we have through His Son's blood is according to the riches of His grace!

Verse 8-10: The "wisdom and prudence" is really connected with "the mystery (secret) of God's will, according to His good pleasure (delight)".

The dispensation of the fulness of times", the heading up of all in the heavens and on earth, is the completion of God's age-long purpose in His Son.

Verse 11: "In Whom also we have obtained an inheritance (Greek *kleroo* = obtaining by lot)." We have obtained an allotment by grace. It was by lot that the Land of Promise was apportioned to the Twelve Tribes of Israel. It is also the case with the Body of Christ with an allotment in the heavenly realms.

"Predestinated according to the purpose of Him Who works all things after the counsel of His own will"; so it is with every member of the Body of Christ. God's foreknowledge preceded His designation beforehand of those He chose (Romans 8:29). But to attempt to understand exactly what determined His choice would be mere presumption, which we would do well to avoid. One treads on holy ground when one talks of God's foreknowledge.

Note that we are not just called to be "saved", but to be conformed to the image of His Son! (Romans 8:29-30). His choice of us shatters all our pride and forbids us to exalt ourselves over our fellow-men!

Verses 12-13: "Who first trusted in Christ" (before hoped in Christ). This verse may be rendered, "Who are in a state of prior expectancy in Christ", our expectation of being manifested with Christ in glory (Colossians 3:1-4). This is prior to Israel's expectation which occurs after the great judgments in the book of Revelation.

"In Whom also after that you believed" (Greek participle "on believing"). There is no interval of time between believing the gospel and being sealed by the Holy Spirit.

Verse 14: This sealing is "the earnest of our inheritance" (allotment); i.e., an installment or, in modern parlance, a down-payment. It is "until the redemption (deliverance) of the purchased possession to the praise of His glory".

Verse 15: "Your faith in the Lord Jesus". Literally, in the Greek, this is "having heard of the according to your faith in the Lord Jesus". This is not good English yet it is something more than simple "faith in". It seems to denote a special faith – a faith associated with the Lord Jesus in His humiliation and death.

Some versions omit the word "love", e.g. *RV*, but in the margin of that version it is stated "many ancient authorities insert the word love."

In the following verses, 17-23 Paul invokes a prayer to lead the saints on to realise the heavenly glories of Christ Jesus.

Verse 17: "A Spirit of wisdom and revelation", which is God given rather than acquired, is vital for a realization (intimate knowledge) of Him.

"The eyes of the heart" are neither the intellect nor the emotions. The heart in Scripture refers to the inmost motives of a person (Proverbs 4:23). We saints have cleansed hearts (2 Timothy 2:22; pure = cleansed). It is these hearts that need to be enlightened by the Holy Spirit.

Verse 18: All this is needed that we may know "the hope (expectation) of His calling". What we are looking forward to in the heavenly realms in Christ, following our upward call to the heavens (Philippians 3:14).

Let us consider Israel who were called by God to bring blessing, both spiritual and material, to the rest of mankind – and will do so both on this earth, during the 1000 years reign of Christ (Revelation

20:6; Isaiah 2:2-3; 11:6-9; Jeremiah 31:31-34; Zechariah 8:5; Matthew 19:28), and on the new earth (Revelation 21:1-4. 10, 14; 22:3-6).

May not the Body of Christ, "blessed with every spiritual blessing" in the heavenly realms, perform a similar function among the heavenly hosts, in Christ? (Note Colossians 1:20).

"The riches of the glory (glorious riches) of His inheritance (Greek *kleronomos* = allotment) among the saints". Our riches as the Body of Christ in the heavenly realms may be contrasted to Israel's on earth, in the Land of Promise. We will be privileged to serve in Christ among the highest strata of heavenly society! Our riches will be the prestige and honour of such service.

Verses 19-20: "The exceeding greatness of His power". Many seek to isolate this statement from its context and make it a prayer for service. We need to believe what God's mighty power has done for Christ in raising Him from the dead and exalting Him to God's right hand. Many rejoice in Christ raised from the dead. O that they may also rejoice in the ascended and seated Christ. May they rejoice also, in appreciating that we are in Him raised and seated at God's right hand.

Verses 21-23: Christ is seated "far above" (Greek *huperano* = up over) all principalities, powers, might and dominion, and every name that is named, not only in this age but also in that which is to come. This is Christ's exaltation, but He does not enjoy this exaltation alone. He is also Head over all to the church (Greek *ecclesia* = His called out ones), which is His Body, the fulness (complement) of Him Who fills (completes) the all in all, the entire Universe.

Christ needs executives to rule on this earth. They will be His chosen people Israel. He also needs executives to rule with Him in the heavenly realms. It is in that sense we are His complement.

Ephesians 2

Ephesians 2

Verse 1: There is a difficulty in translation here. The *KJV* and many versions state that "we were dead *in* trespasses and sins", which is of course true. In the Greek there is no preposition before "trespasses and sins", but the nouns are in the dative case. Paul uses the expression "dead *to* sin" in Romans 6:2, 10-11. Colossians 2:13 and Ephesians 2:1, 5 have the same grammatical construction. This is much more likely what Paul meant than "dead *in* sins". If we are right in this, then if follows that we are "dead to sins" (the root) and "dead to sins" (the fruit).

This is our gracious position in Christ. As we walk in the Spirit (Galatians 5:16-18), we experience the truth. Alas, we do not always walk in the Spirit. Nevertheless the victory is ours in Christ Jesus when we do. Moreover, the Greek present participle is used and the verse should be rendered "*Being* dead to trespasses (offences) and sins".

Verse 2: "According to the course of this world" (Greek *aion* = age or eon. Satan and his minions are the rulers of the lower heavens (the air). He is "the god of this age" (2 Corinthians 4:4). He operates in the "children of disobedience" (sons of willful unbelief, stubbornness), opposing the gracious purpose of God.

Verse 3: "We". The apostle turns from "you", those he is writing to, and includes all the members of Christ's Body. Once we lived "in the lust of our flesh, fulfilling the desires (wills" margin *KJV*) of the flesh and mind (both the coarse and refined desires). Thus we were by nature children of wrath (appointed to wrath), even as others.

Verse 4: "But God, Who is rich in mercy for His great (vast) love with which He loves us". God's love has no boundaries. "Higher than the heavens above; deeper than the deepest ocean, is our Saviour's love!"

Verses 5-6: "Dead in (to) sins". The Greek grammar is the same as in verse 1. Paul is now speaking collectively, (we), of all the members of Christ's Body. The rich mercy and vast love of God has not only made us "dead to sins", but it has "quickened" (made alive) us together corporately in Christ; "by or in grace are we saved!" Still further, we are raised up together and seated together in the heavenly realms, in Christ!

Verse 7: "That in the ages to come, He might show (display) to the heavenly hosts, the exceeding (transcendent riches of His grace, in His kindness to us in Christ Jesus". Why are we subject to such super-abounding grace? Our blessings in Christ Jesus are not just for our selfish enjoyment, but for His glory and blessing to others! Remember our Savior's words, quoted in Acts 20:35, "It is more blessed to give than to receive".

Verse 8: We are saved by grace, not by faith. Faith is the channel which flows to us the Divine stream of saving grace. Both are God's gifts. The Greek word for gift is *doron* = a present; a votive offering; an oblation – Hebrew *corban;* compare Mark 7:11; Leviticus 1:2. It is not a sin offering, but an approach present to God, seeking His favour. How marvellous it is that God Himself reverses this and approaches us with such a gift to win our favour!

Verses 9-10: "Not of works, lest any man should boast." (Compare Romans 4:4-6; Galatians 2:16).

"His workmanship" (Greek *poiema* = a thing made; produced with effort, object and design.) Hence *God's* achievement.

"Created in Christ Jesus", where there is neither Jew nor Greek, but a new creation (Colossians 3:10-11; 2 Corinthians 5:17).

"Unto good works, prepared (margin *KJV*) by God that we should walk in them". Doctrine is balanced by practice.

Verse 11: In this present dispensation of grace it is difficult for us Gentiles to remember what it would be like not to have direct access to God, but to be cut off from Him. The great barrier of circumcision separated us from Israel, and hence from God.

Verse 12: We were "apart from Christ, aliens from the commonwealth (citizenship) of Israel, strangers (Geek *xenos* = lodger, not of the family; i.e. guests) of the covenants of promise, with no expectation and without God in the world.

Verse 13: "But now" in a new creation in Christ Jesus, where there is neither Jew nor Greek, we who were once afar off are made nigh to God by the blood of Christ! Here it is not so much that as unsaved sinners we were "far off" (which is true), but as to our relationship to Israel, the covenant people of God. At best we were like puppies, dependent upon the crumbs that fell from Israel's table (compare Matthew 15:27; Mark 7:28). Now we can receive our Bread of Life direct from God's hands.

Verse 14: "He is our peace" between saved Jews and saved Gentiles, those who accept the gospel of God's grace.

"The middle wall of partition." This was a stone wall, about three cubits high (approximately six feet), which separated the Court of the Gentiles from that of the Jews in the Jerusalem Temple. To pass over to the other side was death to any Gentile. The cross of Christ broke down this barrier between saved Jews and Gentiles. Both are *one in Spirit.*

Verses 15-18: "The enmity"; the various commandments and ordinances, contained in the law of Moses; the rites and ceremonies, unavailable to Gentiles and which causes enmity between them and the Jews, were abolished by Christ's cross (see, Colossians 2:14-17).

We do not know "Christ after the flesh". We are a new creation (2 Corinthians 5:16-17). We are a new humanity, so peace is made. We are reconciled to God and each other by the cross. Peace is now proclaimed to us "far off" Gentiles and to Jews that were nigh. Access to God for both is through Christ and is in *one Spirit.*

Verse 19: No longer are we strangers (guests) and foreigners (sojourners), but fellow-citizens of the Saints. That is, those who received Paul's gospel and whose destiny is to reign with Christ in the heavenly realms, where our seat of government already exists. (Philippians 3:20).

Verse 20: "The foundation (Greek *themelios*) of the apostles and prophets, Jesus Christ (Christ Jesus) Himself being the chief corner stone". This foundation is laid by God Himself. Christ is also the Head of the corner. (Acts 4:11).

Apart from Old Testament prophets, there were also New Testament ones as well (1 Corinthians 12:28; Ephesians 3:5; 4:11).

Verses 21-22: "In Whom (Christ) all the building (the entire building) fitly framed together (Greek *sun-arm-o-logeo* = connect or join together) is growing into a Holy Temple in the Lord".

Compare John 2:19-21. No longer in this dispensation does God dwell in Temples of bricks and mortar, but in His Son and in the hearts of those who are in Christ, His chosen ones! Our very bodies are temples of God's Holy Spirit (1 Corinthians 6:19-20). What a priceless holy intimacy we have with God. So close!

Remember we are bought with a price. How costly it was! Therefore let us glorify God in body and in spirit! (1 Corinthians 6:20).

Ephesians 3

Ephesians 3

Verse 1: "For this cause" (on this account). To what does Paul refer? He is about to begin a prayer. However, before he does so he gives a summary, in chapter 3:2-13, of the present grace relating to the secret dispensation, which is now in force, and the secret of Christ's Headship, over all in the heavens and on earth.

Verses 2-6: Paul is the Apostle of the Gentiles. We would do well to pay attention to him and "the dispensation of the grace of God" which was given to him for us. There are two mysteries (secrets) revealed: -

> (1) The secret of the Body of Christ, with its wholly heavenly blessings (compare 3:6);

> (2) The secret of Christ Himself (compare 1:9-10).

The secret of Christ Himself had been hinted at in Genesis 3:15, and seems to be confined to the earth and its blessing. It was developed in the promises to Israel in the Old Testament and confirmed in the gospels (Matthew 4:17; Mark 1:14-15; Luke 4:17-21 and Romans 15:8-9).

It was not a secret that the Gentiles would be blessed in association with Israel. However, it was a secret never revealed in the Old Testament (for it was hid in God) that believing Gentiles should be fellow heirs (*joint* heirs or allottees), members of a *joint* Body and *joint* partakers of the promise of life in Christ Jesus (compare 2 Timothy 1:1).

Gentiles today are not joined on to an existing Jewish body, but a new body has been created of the two, and in this there is neither Jew nor Greek! They are not to be blessed with Israel on the earth, but are blessed with every spiritual blessing in the heavenly realms. This heavenly side of the secret of Christ "in other ages, was not made know to the sons of men as it is now revealed unto His holy apostles and prophets, by the Spirit".

Verses 7-9: "Less than the least of all saints". This was no pious rhetoric on the part of Paul. He always felt the enormity of his past life in sin, particularly in the way he treated believers in Christ (Acts 9:1-2; 1 Timothy 1:13-15).

"Unsearchable (untraceable) riches of Christ" (compare Romans 11:33). Riches which cannot be traced or followed out until revealed by God.

"The fellowship (Greek *oikonomia* = literally "home law"; an administration) of the secret". This had been hid in God, as stated before. The secret administration was not revealed in the Hebrew and Greek Scriptures until it was revealed to Paul (Colossians 1:25-26).

Verses 10-13: These verses give another reason for God's choice of us believers, to manifest His wisdom to the principalities and powers in the heavenly realms. This is being done now! Every believer, however weak and feeble in faith, is a witness, even though he may be unconscious of it, to the heavenly powers that be. The witness is to them of God's vast love and grace to such unworthy sinners as we are!

It is also a revelation of God's wisdom in coping with Israel's failure that He then revealed His secret purpose in Christ, relating to the Body of Christ which is "blessed with every spiritual blessing in the heavenly realms".

Paul unselfishly rejoiced in his afflictions because they were for our glory! He was a prisoner, bound, unable to visit his various churches; yet God was demonstrating His power and ability to overrule human might.

Verses 14-19: Paul now begins the prayer he digressed from in verses 2-13. "Unto the Father of our Lord Jesus Christ, of Whom every family in heaven and earth is named".

God has many families in heaven and on earth, both in this age and that which is to come. We tend to be selfish when we see only one family – the Body of Christ, the one to which we belong! God's other families are entitled to blessing, mercy and glory. There are "principalities", (sovereignties); "powers", (authorities); "mights", (powers) and "dominions" (lordships) –

Ephesians 1:21. There are "thrones" – Colossians 1:16; and "angels" (messengers) – 1 Peter 3:22. They are all unseen, and we know practically nothing of them.

In order that "Christ may dwell in our hearts by faith", we need a special strengthening by God's Holy Spirit, in the inner man. This is not a question of the human will, but God's might! Christ is in the heart of every true believer (Galatians 4:6), but to dwell in our hearts in all His fulness, we need God's power. The fulness of Christ is His universal Headship, which we, "grounded in God's love", are to grasp by faith.

It is suggested that the dimensions, breadth, length, depth and height may be the tokens of Christ's love!

Its breadth. Once it seemed that God's love was confined to Israel. Now it is as broad as mankind!

Its length. It exists eternally, before the age times began and long after the consummation, when

God is "all in all" in His creation (1 Corinthians 15:28).

Its depth extends right down to the underworld of spirits, of which we know very little.

Its heights rises up over all the sovereignties and authorities, powers and lordships, in the heavenly realms.

Such is "the love of Christ which passes knowledge". To grasp Christ, as such, by faith is to be "filled with all the fulness of God". Christ is the complement of God Who dwells in Him bodily, and we are complete in Him (Colossians 2:10)!

Verses 20-21: "Now to Him that is able to do exceeding abundantly above all that we ask or think, according to the power that works in us". How often this verse is taken out of context and turned into a prayer for power in service! It relates to the previous verses 14-19. Nevertheless, in any capacity God is able to superabound to us, above all our requests and thoughts.

If we have been able to grasp something of Christ's universal headship and love, let us join in the doxology. "To Him be glory in the church and in Christ Jesus to all generations, for ever and ever" (*RSV*), "of the age of the ages" (Nestle and Marshall, *Greek Interlinear of the Authorised Version*).

Ephesians 4

Ephesians 4

Verses 1-3: Some have said, and I think so too, that Paul first dispenses blessing in Christ Jesus and then entreats a worthy walk in the Lord.

"The vocation wherewith you are called". How can we walk worthily of a calling unless we know what it is? The following instructions and precepts assume the knowledge of the previous chapters and flow from it. If we truly appreciate the graciousness of God's calling, then we have no reason for boasting in ourselves.

Humility, meekness, patience and bearing with each other in love, should be our hall-mark. It is not always easy to "keep the unity of the spirit in the bond of peace" amongst some of our fellow believers. It is sometimes an effort and Paul uses the word "endeavour". If we find it difficult, we need to remember that love is the key (1 Corinthians 13:4-8).

Verses 4-6: The unity of the spirit is defined for us in these verses. The vital word is *one.*

One body in Christ. It is not an organisation of our own manufacture. It is an organism, whose members are placed in the Body, as it pleases Christ. No man can put them in, and no man can put them out! It may not be easy for us to be sure about some, but "the Lord knows them that are His".

One Spirit. The Holy Spirit speaks to us through the written Word of God. God's Holy Spirit dwells in our hearts, giving us conscious communion with Him. Where the Spirit of Christ dwells, God's Holy Spirit makes its abode (Romans 8:9-10).

One hope (expectation) – to be manifested together with Christ in glory (Colossians 3:1-4; Titus 2:13; Philippians 3:20-21). This is indeed our "blessed hope", which we long for eagerly.

One Lord. How many there are who seek to usurp His authority over us and attempt to discipline us by man-made rules and regulations! "As ye have therefore received Christ Jesus, the Lord, so walk in Him, rooted and built up in Him" (Colossians 2:6-23).

One faith. Creeds are many but there is only one faith. What is the unity of this faith? It is "the full knowledge of the Son of God, to mature manhood, to the measure of the stature of the fulness of Christ" (verse 13). What a faith that surpasses all "creeds"!

One baptism. Obviously in Spirit (Romans 6:4; Colossians 2:12). Whatever views we may hold on "water baptism", which portrays a spiritual reality, Spirit baptism is vital. Christ Himself is the Baptiser of all who in their hearts acknowledge Him as Lord and Savior.

One God and Father. God is our Father; Christ is God manifest in human flesh (1 Timothy 3:16); the Holy Spirit is God's Holy Spirit (Ephesians 4:30). There are not three Gods, but three manifestations of *one* God.

Verses 7-13: God's gifts to the Body of Christ were specially endowed apostles, prophets, evangelists, pastors and teachers, from the ascended Christ.

Since the Scriptures are complete, requiring no addition, apostles and prophets have fulfilled their function, but evangelists, pastors and teachers remain today. Their object is to lead sinners to Christ and believers on to maturity and to an appreciation of all spiritual blessings in the heavenly realms and see them as distinct and different from Israel's blessings on earth.

Verses 14-16: "No more children (minors) tossed to and fro, carried about with every wind of doctrine". If we hold fast to our Head Christ, we will not be snared by men who handle the Word of God deceitfully, or by those who do not rightly divide the word of truth (2 Timothy 2:15).

"Being true in love" (there is no Greek word for "speak" as in the *KJV*). Our Head Christ, presides over every member of His Body. We receive sustenance and growth through our Head, Christ, and the written word. This can be compared with the physical body nourished with food by which it grows.

Verses 17-19: "Testify (invoke as witness) in the Lord". Paul now invokes the members of Christ's Body not to walk as other Gentiles walk in the "vanity (emptiness of results) of their mind". This relates to their understanding, or rather moral thinking.

"Their understanding is darkened", because they are alienated (estranged) from the life of God. God is the source of all life for "in Him we live and move and have our being" (Acts 17:28). The estrangement is from the purpose of that life which is to live to His glory.

"The ignorance that is in them" is the want of perception, "because of the blindness (hardness) of their hearts".

"Being past feeling" (hardened) they are given over to "lasciviousness" (licentiousness), immoderation, over-indulgence), to "work uncleanness" (impurity as opposed to holiness) and greediness (covetousness).

Verses 20-32:   Paul having warned the saints against the conduct of the Gentile world of unbelievers, now turns his attention to conduct amongst themselves.

"Putting off the old man" (humanity) is based on the fact that we have been created anew in Christ (2 Corinthians 5:17), to live out what God has already put within us.

The "renewal in the spirit of our mind" is the motive behind our changed lives. "Created in righteousness and true holiness." Contrast this with the old Adam, created in the image of God (Genesis 3).

"Speak every man truth with his neighbour". These are the same words as Zechariah 8:16. Lying and deceit belong to the old humanity. (Compare Colossians 3:9.

"Righteousness anger" (indignation) can often be followed by sin. It should speedily give way to peace and no grudge be held against the one who has hurt our feelings. In this way we manifest God's peace towards ourselves and do not give the adversary, Satan, a chance to trip us up.

He who has been stealing, must steal no longer, but must work doing something with his own hands, that he may have something to share with those in need" (v 28 *NIV*; compare Acts 20:33-35).

Let us guard our speech. A corrupt or tainted word may misinform or misrepresent others. Rather may our words edify and minister grace.

Bitterness, wrath, anger, clamour, evil speaking and malice are the things that "grieve the Holy Spirit of God whereby ye are sealed unto the day of redemption" (final deliverance).

In their place let us "be kind to one another, tender-hearted, forgiving one another, even as God for Christ's sake has forgiven you".

Ephesians 5

Ephesians 5

Verses 1-2:   God our Father is love to us and wishes us to copy Him, as beloved children, and walk in love to all we come in contact with.

Christ's sacrificial offering to God was "a sweet smelling savour", a burnt offering entirely devoted to God His Father. It was primarily His obedience to the will of God which gave His death such infinite value. Sin and transgression were secondary in His sacrifice. His faith obedience to the will of His Father, was His motive force (John 6:38-40). So it should be for us in our service to God our Father.

Verses 3-7: In these verses some of the cancers of our society are laid bare: fornication (prostitution); uncleanness; covetousness (greed); filthiness (vileness); foolish talking (stupid speaking); jesting (ribaldry); and idolatry, which is a form of covetousness. Because of these things God's wrath will come upon those who so walk –

the children of (sons) of disobedience (stubbornness).

Verses 8-21: God is Light as well as Love. We should behave as children of light and walk in it, not in darkness (compare John 8:12). Just as in nature, plants respond to light and bear fruit, so should we respond to God's Light and be fruitful. Let us wake up from the lethargy of sleep and "Christ will give us light" (literally, dawn upon us)!

Walk circumspectly (like a cat!). The days in which we live are wicked, ever since Paul wrote this epistle. If we walk in the light of God's will and witness for Him, we are "redeeming the time" (buying up the opportunity), and using the time well to please God (delight Him); compare Philippians 2:13.

A drunkard has no inhibitions. He often abandons himself to raucous and coarse songs. The overflowing of the Spirit in psalms, hymns and spiritual songs, is to be commended.

We have so much to thank God for in our lives! All comes from Him, even things which do not please us! But let us rejoice and thank Him for "He works all things together for good to them that love Him" (Romans 8:28).

Submitting ourselves to one another in the fear (reverence) of the Lord leads us on to domestic relations.

Verses 22-33: "Wives submit (subject) yourselves unto your own husbands, as unto the Lord" (compare Colossians 3:18). This is the only precept given to wives. The feminist advance today would overthrow this divine intention. In the past we have seen the other extreme which reduced a wife to a servile creature, with no mind or will of her own!

However, there is nothing degrading in an intelligent woman being subject to her husband. In fact this is a divine instinct and in a crisis many women instinctively turn to the husbands for help. But also a true husband will always listen to the views and opinions of his wife and put many of them into practice. Many men lean on the wisdom of their wives, though they perhaps do not always admit it! When husbands are loving to their wives, tolerant, sympathetic and understanding, and when wives are subject to their husbands, then there is perfect peace and harmony in their marriage relationships.

Husbands are exhorted to love their wives and be not bitter towards them (Colossians 3:19). Harshness of speech is a wounding thing to a wife and is the direct opposite of love. Love is kind and affectionate and its depth towards the wife is to be like that love our Lord shows to each individual member of His Body. How deep that love is!

No man hates his own flesh, and husband and wife are one flesh (Genesis 2:23-24). So too are the members of Christ's Body – in Spirit. Would Christ ever sever one of His own members, however unworthy and unfaithful? No! So how can husbands contemplate divorcing their own wives? They cannot if they are to love them as Christ loves the members of His Body. How truly great is this secret (verse 32).

Ephesians 6

Ephesians 6

Verses 1-9: Children are given but one, yet far reaching, precept. "Obey your parents in the Lord for this is right". (Compare Colossians 3:20). In the Old Testament, the command to "honour thy father and mother" had the promise of "long life in the Lord" attached to it. In this dispensation, long life is not always given, but God may reward in other ways. Sadly, one of the prevalent signs of our times is the disobedience of children to parents which we not only read and hear about, but which we often see before our own eyes.

Side by side with this goes the exaltation of children over adults. Suffice it to say that the only precept given is "Obey your parents in *all* things for this is well pleasing in the Lord." The Son or daughter who is obedient displays humility, which is the hall-mark of future exaltation, in both the things of this world and in things spiritual.

The sacred duty of fathers, is to nurture their children in the training and admonition of the

Lord. How gracious is that training and admonition! Behind them is a love that will not hesitate to be firm in discipline when necessary. How sickly and sentimental are certain educationalists and psychologists of today, who tell us that children should never be disciplined as it will repress them! We are now seeing some of the fruit of their labours in today's society and some of these poor children are appearing in the juvenile courts.

Fathers must not vex their children. Unfair punishments, insistence on punctilious obedience to unnecessary and niggling rules, sarcasm and biting comment, will discourage children and make them rebellious. Let fathers, by their example and teaching, bring their children up in the reverence of the Lord.

Servants and Masters. In the Western world today, this state of affairs is outmoded, but the principle of obedience to those over us, i.e. management and workers, is still applicable today (compare Colossians 3:22-4:1).

Service should be rendered with proper respect and singleness of heart and as to the Lord. It should not be done with an outward show to please men, but should be done cheerfully. This is not easy, especially when the "boss" is difficult to please, unfair and even harsh. But we are reminded that the Lord will compensate us with the enjoyment of the inheritance (allotment) – compare Colossians 3:24-25 – and that whatsoever good we may do will be requited to us by Him, and the same applies to any injury we may do.

The same principle applies to believing managers as to the workers under them. They are reminded that their master in the heavens requires them to be just and fair to their workers, not given to threatening. We are living in days of strife and strike, lock-out and work-in, antagonism and dispute, but no amount of arbitration or new agreements between employers and employees really solve the problem.

It is only here and there where the believing boss and believing worker work together to practice the truth contained in Ephesians and Colossians that there is harmony and peace, and this makes trade unions and shop stewards superfluous.

Verses 10-17: The heavenly conflict and the Armour of God. [2] When Israel occupied the Promised Land, they frequently had to defend it against the nations they had displaced. When faith in the Lord and obedience to His will prevailed, they were victorious over their adversaries. When they departed from following the Lord, they were defeated. On such occasions He raised up men of faith and valour. Men who, by faith obedience, led the nation of Israel once more to overcome their enemies. The book of Judges is full of such names – Gideon, Deborah and Barak, Samson, etc.,

We, like Israel, have a *Promised Land*, not on earth but in the heavenly realms. But the principalities, powers, and rulers of the darkness of this age (verse 12) very much resent our intrusion into their realm. Hence, there is need for

---

[2] For a more detailed treatment of The Armour of God see the book *The Armour of God* by James Poole, published by The Open Bible Trust.

Divine Armour to protect us in our conflict with them, as they seek to prevent us from enjoying by faith God's inheritance (allotment) among the saints in Christ Jesus. Now, how can we hold on to our heavenly allotment? We need "to be strong in the Lord and the power of His might."

The power of His might consists in an armour or panoply and if we put it on it provides us with complete protection from all our spiritual foes. We are living in an evil day (Galatians 1:4) where there is so much departure from the faith once delivered to the saints. These evil powers attack us through our sinful flesh, through other human beings and sometimes, sadly, through fellow believers.

The Belt of Truth.
This covers the waist. Without "truth" we are in darkness and error. Our Lord said "I am the Truth" (John 14:6). The written Word of God points to the Living Word, Christ Jesus our Lord. We must "rightly divide the Word of Truth" (2 Timothy 2:15) to distinguish that which applies to Israel, exclusively, and that which applies to the Body of

Christ. There is much Divine Truth in the whole Bible applicable in all dispensations which the believer can and should apply to himself, for "all Scripture is given by inspiration of God and is profitable for doctrine, for reproof, for correction, for instruction in righteousness; that the man of God may be perfect (complete), thoroughly furnished (equipped) unto all good works" (2 Timothy 3:16-17).

The Breastplate of Righteousness.
This is God's Righteousness which comes to us through faith in Christ and which protects us all round, back and front (Romans 3:22) against the assaults of the Adversary, Satan. We have a righteous standing in Christ before God which does not vary.

However, in order to defeat our spiritual foes, we must live righteously in the power of Christ's resurrection life, or else we shall suffer some wounding by Satan. Unrighteous acts condemn us in the sight of men and our spiritual adversaries. We shall also incur loss at the Judgment Seat of

Christ when our walk and service are assessed by Him. (Romans 14:10; 2 Corinthians 5:10).

The Sandals of Peace.
We are at peace with God (Romans 5:1-2) and in the light of His present reconciliation to mankind, we should imitate Him by "having our feed shod with the preparation of the gospel of peace" towards mankind. Reconciliation is the Greek *katalasso*, conciliate; i.e. one side only. *Apokatalasso* is reconciliate; i.e. both sides.

At present the world is not reconciled to God, but it is conciliated on God's part. When this is received by the sinner, reconciliation takes place, between both God and the sinner. In this dispensation God does not take into account our trespasses (offences) against Him, so we should not take into account mankind's offenses against us (2 Corinthians 5:19).

It is not always easy to adopt such a forgiving attitude towards some of our fellow men, believers and unbelievers. The flesh in us gets irritated so that, alas, at times we do not have on the sandals of peace. This Satan can exploit to his advantage. The more we are conscious of our unworthiness and God's super-abounding grace to ourselves, then the more we are encouraged to be like our heavenly Father and to walk in love (compare 2 Timothy 2:24-26).

The Shield of Faith:
(Greek *thureos)*. This is not a small shield used in hand to hand combat. One could compare it to the large shields used by our riot police against violent mobs that throw things at them. Such a large shield is ours to protect us from the fiery darts of Satan. Note that this is the large shield of *the* faith (the definite article is there in the Greek) that Paul has brought us in his prison epistles. A faith embodied in Christ Jesus, our risen, ascended and seated Lord of Glory. He is our Shield of Faith! He alone can ward off Satan's fiery darts from wounding us. (CF. Psalm 119:14.)

The Helmet of Salvation.
The helmet guards our head (mind). This is mentioned last for it is the last to be put on. Is it not when our Lord is manifested in glory, our

hope, that our salvation will be completed, put on? Then we shall be in His presence in the heavenly realms.

The Sword of the Spirit.
Now clothed in all parts of our spiritual armour, we may be entrusted with a sword, which is the Word of God. Swordplay is an art, a skilled exercise. It is not for the unskilled. God's Word is a defensive weapon against the lies of Satan.

How sad it is to see the unskillful use of God's Word by some saints who, instead of using it against the lies of Satan, hack each other about! The sword is to be used against wicked spirits, not our fellow human beings; (compare verse 12). If you want to see a Master Swordsman at work, turn to Matthew 4:1-11. Notice the way our Lord parried the sword thrusts of Satan. "It is written" was the reply to all Satan's thrusts.

Verses 18-24: There remains one more vital thing – prayer. Each part of the armour should be put on with prayer. The Ephesian saints and others were requested by Paul to pray for him and his ministry and for all the saints. He asked for boldness to make known the secret of the Gospel of peace (verse 15), which is God's peace promoting attitude to a world of sinners, and the secret administration relating to the Body of Christ with its heavenly destiny. All those today who seek to make known these precious truths need our prayers. (2 Corinthians 5:18-21, Ephesians 1:3.)

Let us consider Paul's closing benediction to this glorious epistle to the Ephesians. "Peace to the brethren and love with faith from God the Father and the Lord Jesus Christ" (verse 23). What a soothing word is "peace". There is the peace that our heavenly Father gives us and bids us to show to our fellow men (verse 15 and 2 Corinthians 5:18-21). There is also "the peace of God, which passes all understanding, which guards our hearts and minds in Christ Jesus" (Philippians 4:7). Such peace is superior to every other frame of mind.

"Grace be with all those who love our Lord in sincerity (incorruption). Amen." Let us love "all who call on the Lord out of a cleansed heart". We do not all see eye to eye with other Christians. We may not have the same understanding of God's Word. However, if we truly love our Lord in the light of the truth God has revealed to us, may God's grace abound to all of us!

Conclusion

Conclusion

I realise that I have given a few random notes on this magnificent epistle. Ephesians reveals to us the very zenith of our risen Lord's glory. I feel that I have only scratched its surface and there are many more nuggets of gold to be dug out, but what I have dug out, I rejoice in and long to pass on to others! However, may the Lord overrule any errors on my part and bless that which accords with the Holy Spirit.

———————————

More on Ephesians

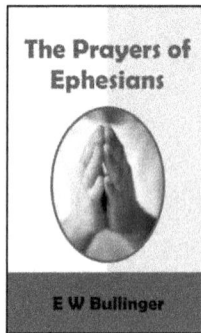

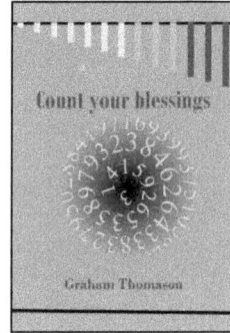

Spiritual Blessing in heavenly realms
Brian Sherring
Using Ephesians 1:3 as his starting point the author brings before the reader the spiritual blessing Paul goes on to write about.

The Prayers of Ephesians
E W Bullinger
This deals with the major prayers of chapters 1 & 3, and Paul's comments on prayer at the end of chapter 6.

Count your blessing
Graham Thomason
This majors on the blessing Christians have in Christ, many of which Paul wrote about in Ephesians

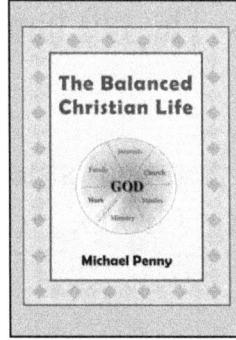

Sit, Walk, Stand
The Christian life in Ephesians
W M Henry and Michael Penny

- What have Christian in Christ that they can rest upon (Sit)?
- How should they live their lives (Walk)?
- What must they resist (Stand)?

The Balanced Christian Life
Michael Penny
A series of five studies based on Ephesians exploring …

The Blessings Christians have in Christ and The Practical Christian Life which should follow

This is a large book designed for individual or group work. The right hand pages ask questions, fill in Bible quotations and other open ended activities. The left hand pages contain the answers.

Ideal for personal study and for any Lent Group, Post Alpha Group, House Group or Bible Study Group.

If any organisations wish to use the diagrams and worksheets contained in this book they are free to copy them, and there is no need to seek permission.

That you may be filled
Charles Ozanne
The aim of this book is to investigate the unsearchable riches of Christ as found in Paul's most exalted epistle, Ephesians. By selecting some of the more significant passages Charles Ozanne has brought to light the unique message of this epistle.

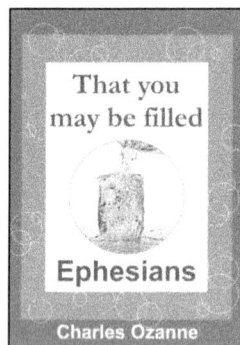

The author's hope is that having read this publication the reader will have a deeper understanding and a higher appreciation of God's purpose for this age of grace

Further details of all the books here can be seen
on **www.obt.org.uk**

The can be ordered from the website
and also from

The Open Bible Trust,
Fordland Mount, Upper Basildon,
Reading, RG8 8LU, UK.

They are also available as eBooks
from Amazon and Apple,
and also as KDP paperbacks from Amazon.

Free sample

About the author

James Poole was born in Finchley, London, in 1909 and took a course in Business Training at the City of London College. During his working years he was employed by various institutions and banks in the City of London. When he wrote this booklet he was enjoying retirement with his wife in Eastbourne, Sussex, but has since fallen asleep in Christ.

Also by James Poole

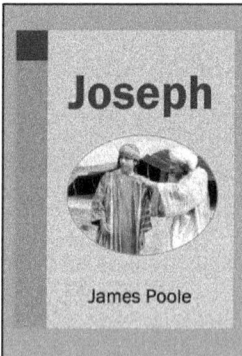

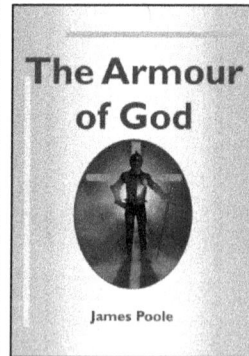

Abraham

James Poole

Isaac

James Poole

Jacob

James Poole

Joseph

James Poole

Notes on Ephesians

James Poole

The Armour of God

James Poole

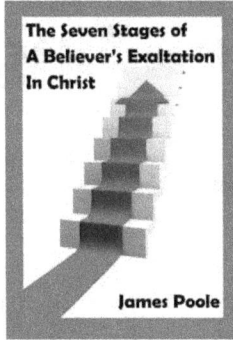

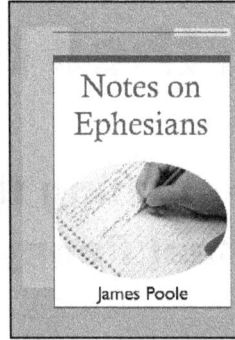

Further details of all the books here can be seen
on **www.obt.org.uk**

The can be ordered from the website
and also from

The Open Bible Trust,
Fordland Mount, Upper Basildon,
Reading, RG8 8LU, UK.

They are also available as eBooks
from Amazon and Apple,
and also as KDP paperbacks from Amazon.

Further Reading

Approaching the Bible
Michael Penny

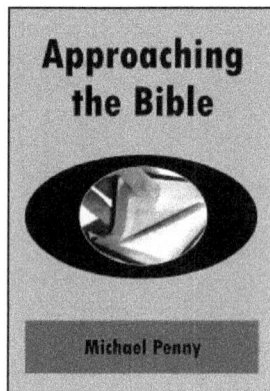

In easy to understand steps, and with many interesting examples, Michael Penny provides the rational for the view that before we try to *apply* any passage in the Bible to ourselves, we should discover first what it meant to those to whom its words were initially addressed. The book advocates that this is best done by considering the passage under the following headings:

1) **W**ho said or wrote it;
2) to **W**hom was it said or written, or concerning **W**hom was it said or written;
3) **W**here it was said or written, or concerning **W**here was it said or written;
4) **W**hat was said or written;
5) **W**hen was it said or written, or concerning **W**hen was it said or written;
6) **W**hy was it said or written.

Applying these six **"W"** rules puts the passage into its proper context and gives us the right perspective on it. Only after doing this can we determine:

7) **W**hether the passage applies to our situation and what the correct application is.

It is the *consistent* use of these **Seven Ws** which helps us discover the right and relevant application of any passage to our lives.

****

This book, and the one on the next page, can be ordered from **www.obt.org.uk** and from

The Open Bible Trust,
Fordland Mount, Upper Basildon,
Reading, RG8 8LU, UK.

40 Problem Passages
Michael Penny

This book is a sequel to *Approaching the Bible*.

The 7 Ws advocated in *Approaching the Bible* are applied to 40 difficult to understand passages. There are, of course, far more than 40 Problem Passages in the Bible. However, in this book Michael Penny not only solves these *40 Problem Passages*, but in doing so he equips the reader with a method by which many, many more hard to understand and difficult passages can be understood and successfully applied to the life of the believer today.

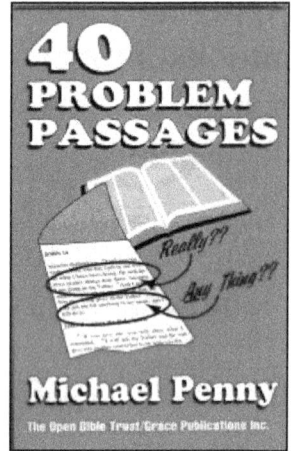

****

This book, and the ones on the previous pages, are also available as eBooks from Amazon and Apple,

and also as KDP paperbacks from Amazon.

About this Book

Notes on Ephesians

An excellent, short introduction to the letter many consider to be Paul's greatest.

The author places Ephesians in its historical setting. He then gives short and clear notes on many verses. These bring to life what Paul wrote those many centuries ago, and which are so relevant to Christians of the 21st Century.

Publications of The Open Bible Trust must be in accordance with its evangelical, fundamental and dispensational basis. However, beyond this minimum, writers are free to express whatever beliefs they may have as their own understanding, provided that the aim in so doing is to further the object of The Open Bible Trust. A copy of the doctrinal basis is available on **www.obt.org.uk** or from:

THE OPEN BIBLE TRUST
Fordland Mount, Upper Basildon,
Reading, RG8 8LU, UK.

www.ingramcontent.com/pod-product-compliance
Lightning Source LLC
Chambersburg PA
CBHW060655030426
42337CB00017B/2634